Dedication :
To all the "Earth Angels" who have supported me on my own journey, including Brian, Ray, Richard, Trudi and many others xx

"This time, I think I can do it!" said Daphne the little dolphin to herself trembling with fear. She tried to steady herself on her surfboard as the next wave rolled towards her, bigger, and bigger.

"Here goes." Daphne thought nervously as her surf board began to wobble, and then, like so many times before….sploosh! She fell in the water again.

As she came up to the surface, Daphne could hear some of her friends laughing at her whilst her teacher, he simply shook his head. Daphne headed for home.

"I'm confused." she muttered to herself, trying not to cry,
"I thought friends were supposed to be kind."

She was so deep in thought, that she almost swam into the mouth of a great big basking shark and jumped out of her skin!

"Why is the world so scary?"

Daphne groaned, and swam on home as fast as she could.

A few days later, Daphne's mum was fed up of her moping about, so she sent her off to see her grandad.

"Now, what's all this I hear about you getting under your mother's fins and being miserable?" grandad asked her.

Daphne looked down at the seabed.

"Come on." said grandad "It can't be that bad."

"Yes it can!" said Daphne defiantly, "I'm no good at school, I'm too clumsy to learn to surf so my friends all laugh at me, and well, I'm frightened in case the big creatures pick on me as well!"

Grandad thought for a moment. "Well." he said at last, "I used to feel a bit like that when I was your age, but then I went to see my grandad."

"What happened?" asked Daphne.

Grandad smiled, "He taught me a very useful trick and I still use it, even today."

Daphne felt herself cheering up. "What is it? What's the trick?"

Grandad pointed to a shelf, where he kept a glass jar with shells in it. No ordinary shells, but shells with smiley faces painted on them.

Daphne had often wondered about the smiley shells, but never had the courage to ask about them. They looked so pretty and lots of fun!

"That's my **bank a smile jar**." said grandad. Just hearing the name made Daphne smile.

"This is how it works." said grandad lifting the jar down from the shelf. "Every evening after tea, I sit down and think of at least five good things about me. It could be things I've done, or it could just be something I like about myself."

"What five things will you think today grandad?"

Grandad looked at Daphne for a moment. "Well, today I'm enjoying spending time with you. Ooh, this morning I helped old Jimmy Jellyfish get untangled from a plastic bag that some human being had thrown into the sea. Remember, you can include things you would like to come true too."

Daphne's eyes grew wide. "Really, you can wish things to be true?"

"Oh yes" said grandad "You see, it's a question of learning to believe in yourself." Daphne trusted her grandad, so she listened carefully to what he said next.

"Just say **I'm happy that** about something you want to be true. That's not so very difficult is it?"

Daphne looked across at the jar again and giggled, because all the shells were smiling back at her.

"What do you do when the jar gets full?" Daphne asked.

"Recycle my girl, recycle! I take them out and I start all over again."

Daphne laughed out loud. "I love you grandad!"

"Quite so, and I love you too. Now, it's time to celebrate. How about one of your grandma's seaweed muffins?"

Back at home with a pocket full of smiley shells her grandad had given her, Daphne asked her mum if she could have an empty jar. Her mum didn't ask what the jar was for, she was just happy that Daphne looked less down in the dumps.

The first shell was easy. "I'm so happy that I told grandad how I was feeling."

Plink! The shell hit the bottom of the jar.

She pondered for a while "I know! I'm happy that I painted a smiley face on my **"bank a smile jar**."

Plink! Another shell landed in the bottom of the jar.

Then she tidied her bedroom and put another shell in the jar. That felt good!

The next day at school Daphne felt a little bit more confident and she didn't even mind too much when her friends laughed at her as she tried to surf. That evening, Daphne thought about why she was feeling a bit better.

"I'm happy that I'm not so scared of the shadows." she began and put a shell in the jar. After a few more moments she picked up another shell.

"I'm happy that...I've got nice flippers!" Plink!

Then she remembered about saying things she would like to be true. She carefully chose a big shell with a very happy smile on it. "I'm happy that I'm brave and I'm happy that I can surf!" And she thought how wonderful it was skipping along on top of the waves.

Daphne carried on with the smiley shells. She had good days and days that weren't quite so good, until gradually she noticed the dolphins that she thought were her friends didn't come to play with her any more but she had new friends who were much more fun to be with.

Her teacher told her he could see she was really making great progress and even the bigger dolphins and sea creatures...they just didn't seem scary any more!

Daphne was even happy spending time on her own surfing the waves and collecting more shells to take home.

Daphne realised, just as grandad had promised, that by believing she could be happy she really was happy!

THE END

Make Your Own Smiley Shells.....

1) Decorate a jar, a plastic cookie tub or even a sandwhich box will do. Customise your jar with stickers, ribbons or paints and you could put your name on it too.

2) Collect shells from the beach or if you prefer use milk or water bottle lids or large buttons or even pieces or card cut into circles. Put smiley stickers on them or paint on a smiley face.
As you take each shell say "I am so happy that........" and pop a **shell** in your jar. Think of as many things as you can.

3) Encourage your child to think of something they can like about themselves. This could be their smile, their eyes, their voice, that they enjoy dancing or listening to music or perhaps have a favourite song they enjoy singing along to and that they appreciate their favourite toy and so on. (If they are unsure tell them something you like about them, then get them to choose something as well.)

4) Encourage your child to think of some things they have done well today. Did they clean their teeth? Did they put their toys away? Draw or play nicely with a friend? Again they may need some reminding but it's important for them to say what they are proud of. This is a good time to reinforce positive behaviour.

5) Allow your child to think of something they would like to happen. An afternoon down at the beach, learning a new skill, having a friend round for tea, what they will be when they grow up or anything else that makes them feel happy. Encourage them to imagine themselves in that scene - what are they seeing, doing, hearing, feeling? This will help them move faster towards their goals and look forward to fun things.